I0440789

Copyright 2015 Jane Konz.

ISBN-13:978-1508726319

CONTENT.

A   is for Australia.

B   is for Back-young.

C   is for Claws.

D   is for Doze.

E   is for Enemies.

F   is for Fur.

G   is for Gumtrees.

H   is for Home Range.

I   is for Illness.

J   is for Joey.

K   is for Koala.

L   is for Leaves.

M   is for Movement.

N   is for Nocturnal.

O   is for Opposable.

P   is for Pouch.

Q   is for Quiet.

R   is for Rescue and Rehabilitation.

S   is for Scats.

T   is for Teeth.

U   is for Urbanisation.

V   is for Vulnerable.

W   is for Water.

X   is for X-Factor.

Y   is for You.

Z   is for Zoo.

Koala Groups.

 **is for Australia.**

It is the only country in the world where Koalas are found in the wild.
They only live on the eastern side of the country in the states of Queensland, New South Wales, Victoria, South Australia and the Australian Capital Territory. These states are the areas where their food trees are in greater numbers.

B is for Back-Young.

A term used for a young Koala aged between about 6 -12 months. The young Koala will hitch a ride on its mothers back as it begins to explore the world. This enables the mother to move more freely around the trees and the youngster remains safe.

C is for Claws.

Koalas have long sharp, strong curved claws. They need these for climbing. Claw marks can be found on the trunks of trees Koalas use regularly.

There is no claw on the big toe of their back paws and the 2nd and 3rd toes are fused together to make a grooming claw.

D is for Doze.

Koalas spend 18 hours a day in the forks of trees dozing. They have to do this because their diet is low in energy and their metabolism is slow. In cold weather they can be seen curled up in a ball, in hot weather they are sprawled out with limbs hanging.

 **is for Enemies.**

The Koalas natural enemies are Dingoes, Wild Dogs and Foxes. Young Koalas can also fall prey to Goannas, Wedge Tail Eagles and certain Owls. However the biggest enemy to the Koala are Humans, their pet dogs and cars.

 **is for Fur.**

Koala's fur coats are different depending on the climate they live in. The bigger southern Koalas fur is long and shaggy to protect it from the cold winters. In the warmer north, Koalas are small with shorter fur.

The colour varies from grey to brown becoming much lighter on their stomach. Their fur repels water to protect them in the rain.

 **is for Gum Tree.**

Gum Trees as they are commonly known in Australia are Eucalyptus trees. There are over 600 different species, although Koalas only eat the leaves from about 40-50, preferring only a few local to their habitat. Whilst the Koala is a protected species the trees they depend on for food and shelter are not.

 **is for Home Range.**

This is the name for the
territory of an individual
Koala. It includes their food
and shelter trees.
Although they are solitary
animals, you will rarely see a
wild Koala sharing a tree,
they live within societies, side
by side, like an overlapping
jigsaw puzzle.
In healthy Habitat they rarely
leave their Home Range.

I is for Illness.

Koalas are affected by Chlamydia. Symptoms are Cystitis, which makes their bottoms look wet and dirty. Conjunctivitis, which makes their eyes red, swollen and can cause blindness. In females it can leave them infertile.

Also Retrovirus a HIV type of immune disorder that can lead to Leukaemia and Lymphoma.

 **is for Joey.**

The term used for a baby Koala. After 35 days gestation they are born the size of a jelly bean, pink, with no fur and their ears and eyes still closed. They are called a 'Pinkie'. They pull themselves through their mothers' fur to her pouch where they stay for the next six months. At about 4 months when they have fur they begin to peep out at the outside world.

 **is for Koala.**

The Koala is a Mammal, Marsupial and Herbivore. Male Koalas have longer broader faces, a scent gland on their chest and can weigh up to 12kg. Females are smaller, prettier with softer faces, fluffy ears and can weigh up to 8kg. A healthy Koala can live till 18 years old. This is much less in the wild. When curled up they're about the size of a basketball.

L is for Leaves.

A Koala survives almost totally on a daily diet of Eucalyptus leaves. An adult eats around 500 -750gms. Although poisonous to other animals, Koalas have an especially adapted digestive system.
They will also eat the bark, buds and flowers.
To supplement their mineral intake they occasionally snack on dirt!

 **is for Movement.**

Koalas either climb up and down trees using the opposite arm to leg, or bound up quickly using their strong hind legs to push. They descend bottom first.
In the trees they jump from branch to branch using their strong sense of balance and co-ordination.
On the ground they walk on all fours in an awkward looking motion.

N is for Nocturnal.

Koalas sleep most of the day, so it's at night when they are most active. This is when they spend most of their time eating and moving from tree to tree. This is also the time they are in most danger as once on the ground they are at risk from predators.

O is for Opposable.

Koalas have five digits on each front paw. Two of them are opposable rather like a Human thumb. This makes it easier for them to grip and climb trees.
They are also the only other mammal other than Primates to have fingerprints.

 **P** **is for Pouch.**

Female Koalas have a downward facing pouch, which they can close like a drawstring bag with specially developed muscles. The pouch is home to a Joey for about 6 months. It has 2 teats, one of which the Joey attaches itself to as soon as it crawls inside. The teat swells to fit the Joeys mouth so it cannot become detached from its food supply.

 **is for Quiet.**

Koalas are thought of as silent. However they do make a variety of sounds.
Males make a bellowing sound like a loud snore and burp to attract females!
Females murmur and softly click to their young. Joeys make a yipping noise to call their mothers.
All make a sound like a screaming baby when in extreme stress.

 **is for Rescue &**

Rehabilitation.

Along the east coast of Australia there are a number of Rescue and Rehabilitation centres which devote their time to nursing sick and injured Koalas back to health. A lot of these also have home carers who hand rear orphaned Joeys. The majority of these are staffed by volunteers and have to raise their own funds.

 **S** **is for Scats.**

Scats are the term used for Koala poo! They are small bullet shaped pellets that smell of eucalyptus. A healthy Koala will do up to 180 Scats a day! Koala Scats give an indication to the state of their health.

If you are looking for wild Koalas check around the bottom of a Eucalypt tree for Scats as this will show you if a Koala is in that area.

T is for Teeth.

Koalas have strong sharp teeth. The front ones are for clipping leaves, the back ones for chewing. There is a small gap between their front and back teeth which allows them to move their tongue around their mouth to move the leaves.

A Koalas age is told by the state of its teeth. The older the Koala the more worn down their back teeth are.

U is for Urbanisation.

As more and more houses and roads are built Koala habitat is destroyed. So far over 80% has been lost. Corridors, which are areas of vegetation linking patches of bush, are being cut by development. This means Koalas have to travel on the ground in search of food and mates. They are then in extreme danger from dog attacks and traffic accidents.

 is for Vulnerable.

Vulnerable means that
although the Koala is not
listed as endangered it
recognises that numbers are
continuing to drop.
 After advice received from
the Threatened Species
Scientific Council, the Federal
Environment Minister, in April
2012, listed Koalas in NSW,
Queensland and the ACT as
vulnerable.

 **is for Water.**

The word Koala is thought to have originated from an Aboriginal word for No Drink. Koalas generally get most of their liquid intake from the moisture in Eucalypt leaves. However in drought or extreme circumstances like bushfires they will drink water.

 **is for X-Factor.**

As an Australian icon, Koalas have this in abundance. They are one of Australia's biggest tourist attractions. Most tourists state that Koalas are the thing they want to see when visiting Australia.

They are the animal, [Fauna], emblem for the state of Queensland and appear as regular stars on Australian stamps and collectable coins.

 **is for You.**

There are many things YOU can do to help the Koala survive.
If you live in a Koala area, please stop your dogs roaming, especially at night and take care on the roads between dusk and dawn.
Donate time or money to a Koala organisation.
If you are from overseas please make a donation, sponsor a Koala or join an organisation as an overseas member.

Z is for Zoo.

Zoos play an important role in the survival of the Koala.
They have conservation and breeding programmes, ensuring there will be Koalas for future generations.
Those with wildlife hospitals provide expert care for sick and injured Koalas.
They are a place for tourists to go, to see, cuddle and photograph Koalas.

Koala Groups.

Australian Koala Foundation. Brisbane, Qld.
www.savethekoala.com

Friends of the Koala Inc. East Lismore, NSW.
www.friendsofthekoala.org

Koala Preservation Society and Koala Hospital.
Port Macquarie, NSW.
www.koaalahospital.org.au

Hunter Koala Preservation Society. Tanilba Bay NSW
www.hunterkoala.com

Koala Action Group Qld Inc. Capalaba, QLD.
www.koalagroup.asn.au

Moreton Bay Koala Rescue. Burpengary, QLD.
www.moretonbaykoalarescue.org

Ipswich Koala Protection Society.
Mount Forbes, QLD.
www.ikps.com.au

Sunshine Coast Koala Wildlife Rescue.
Myrtle Beach, QLD.
www.sckoalarescue.com.au

Koalas in Care Inc. Taree, NSW.
www.koalasincare.org.au

Pine Rivers Koala Care Assoc Inc.
Strathpine, QLD.
www.prkoalacare.com.au

Southern Ash Wildlife Shelter. Rawson, VIC.
www.samthekoala.com.au

www.ingramcontent.com/pod-product-compliance
Lightning Source LLC
Chambersburg PA
CBHW050837290526
45792CB00001B/433